Maze *of* Thorns

KRIS KELBRANTS & SHERRY SHUSS

Maze of Thorns
by Kris Kelbrants and Sherry Shuss
Copyright ©2016 Kris Kelbrants and Sherry Shuss

First edition

Healthy Angel Press
Apple Valley, Minnesota 55124

Visit us at MyHealthyAngel.com

ISBN: 978-0-692-76204-2

Printed in the United States of America

Dedication

This is for our husbands, who encouraged and supported us through endless hours of writing.

Contents

1. Enter the Maze 1

2. A Tangled Web 5

3. Blind Alley 11

4. Flight 15

5. Spiraling Down 19

6. Dark Passageways 25

7. Bleak Tunnel 31

8. Hanging By a Thread 37

9. The Vortex 49

10. A Fork in the Road 77

11. Center of the Labyrinth 93

12. Final Thoughts - Kris. 105

13. Final Thoughts - Sherry 115

    About the Authors 118

Acknowledgements

As we finish our journey, we wish to thank Dr. Ridley, Dr. Penovich, Shelly Wick and all the hospital staff for going above and beyond.

We wish to thank our family and friends. We were blessed with incredible support in so many different ways. Everyone had their strengths and special contributions. We survived this only because of the love everyone shared and we hope each one of you knows what a special role you played.

We want to thank our editor, Bonnie McDermid, and Joy Pecchia, who introduced us to Bonnie and encouraged us to start this journey.

Kris: A special thanks to Dr. Ridley. I've now known Dr. Ridley for over 19 years. There have been ups and downs and flare-ups with my illness and through it all, Dr. Ridley has kept me alive and fighting for the good life.

Sherry: Blessings to my friends, Sharon and Lana, who were by my side at the hospital, each providing comfort and support in her own way.

Kris: I would like to thank my friends Janna and Tifani for the countless hours they spent helping me, both in the hospital and after. Finally, I would like to acknowledge Oliver, my lifelong companion, who gave me 17½ years of unconditional love.

And most of all, we wish to thank our God. With Him, all things are possible.

The fall before it all happened. Sherry, Roger & Kris

Introduction

Our daughter had a sudden health condition that changed all of our lives. This is the story of how an illness that is virtually a death sentence can break you down, reach into the depths of your soul and turn your life upside down. It is a story that tested our faith because we had to give up all control.

Prior to her illness, our daughter was a powerhouse. She had run two marathons, was a fitness instructor and had worked for two major corporations. Life was sweet.

Then out of the blue, Kris became very ill. Every day we searched for answers that would lead us out of the maze.

When the unthinkable happens and you're not strong enough alone—what do you do then?

Though the Lord brings grief,
he will show compassion,
so great is his unfailing love.

Lamentations 3:32

Chapter 1
Enter the Maze

MARCH
KRIS

I first noticed it at work: while editing my company's publications, I would read the same sentences over and over again, but not comprehend them.

My mind is racing so fast that I can't focus.

I am exhausted. To make it through the day, I am drinking Mountain Dew and eating candy, even though I'm not hungry. This is not like me. Never in a million years do I eat junk all day—I eat healthy.

I have this tight feeling in my jaw and a metallic taste in my mouth that I can't seem to shake.

I am worried I can't do my job. I went back to review the training manuals from my first few weeks on the job, but even those are confusing.

What if someone realizes that I'm not getting anything done? Maybe I should quit before they figure it out?

MARCH
SHERRY

Kris stopped over to visit today and, out of the blue, told us she needs to quit her job. She kept repeating, "If I don't quit, I'll be fired," but couldn't explain why.

I'm certain she can find another job, but I just can't understand why it is so urgent that she quit immediately. Usually, she thinks things through and has a Plan B. Kris is a planner; nothing happens without her making a plan and reviewing it several times. And now she just wants to quit with no other job prospects on the horizon?

Her dad and I just don't function like that. You don't leave one job until you have another one. You make plans and then follow through. We didn't help pay for college and she didn't work so hard just to quit. While we are not in favor of her quitting this job until she has a new one, we also know her abilities will make it possible to find something new and better to do.

But there is no arguing with her. From the age of two, Kris could "do it myself." She handles things on her own and never takes anyone into her confidence when she needs help.

APRIL 9
KRIS

Today, I resigned from my job with a one-sentence letter. I had to quit because I can't do my job anymore. I told my parents I planned to quit my job before resigning but, as usual, I wasn't open to much discussion about it.

At least that part of my life seems normal.

APRIL 9-15
KRIS

After I quit my job, I retreated to my apartment. There, I floated from day to day without much thought as to what I should be doing or what needed to be done. I watched television, but couldn't follow the story lines. I didn't work out and, for once, didn't feel any guilt. This is surely not characteristic; I rarely miss a workout or sit still through an entire television program.

Somebody brought me the book, *You Can Make It Happen Every Day* by Stedman Graham. I would pick up the book and see the words, but couldn't make sense of them. Out of frustration, I would put the book down and go back to staring at the television. (I learned much later the book was from my mom, an effort to motivate me out of my "depression.")

One day, in a flash of clarity, I realized something was terribly wrong. In a panic and crying, I called my good friend, Tifani, who dropped everything and drove a half-hour to be with me.

I wasn't aware of how much time passed while I sat in that apartment—it seemed like an eternity. But just one week after my resignation, I took my first step into the hospital.

It was like stepping into a maze of thorns. From that moment forward, I had only momentary glimpses of reality.

To the land of deepest night,
of deep shadow and disorder,
where even the light is like darkness.

Job 10:22

Chapter 2
A Tangled Web

APRIL 9-15
SHERRY

Since Kris quit her job, she has been spending all of her time alone in her apartment, away from us. When we visit her, she is so distant, unemotional and unresponsive that we can't even have a conversation with her. To get her interested in going back to work, I gave her a book.

Her dad and I think maybe she is depressed—but why? Doing nothing is just not in her makeup.

Out of the blue, Kris' friend, Tifani, called to say she was very concerned about Kris; she had rushed down to be with her during a full-scale panic attack.

Then today, Kris asked me, "Why are you freaking out about my having a job when I'm dying?"

What is this all about? Is she really sick and is this serious? I mean, she looks good, acts like she is fine and hasn't shared any of these feelings before.

But because her behavior is so strange and out of character, I think we might need professional help, so I made an appointment next week with a psychologist at the hospital.

APRIL 16
The day you were admitted to the mental health unit
ANN

I drove you to your first appointment, a group counseling session. Shortly after the session began, the counselor brought you back to me in the waiting room. She told me that you needed more help than they could give you in the group session.

Then she asked you if you had thought about taking your life.

"Yes," you replied.

"Do you have a plan?" she asked.

"Yes," you replied.

"Can you tell us the plan?"

You said, "There is a block of knives in my parents' kitchen. I'm going to stab myself in the kitchen. It will be easy to clean up the floor in there."

The counselor then told me it would be best for you to be admitted to the mental health unit and asked me to call your mom. As I went to call, you told me to ask your mom to bring Leo. I called your mom at work and told her about the conversation with the counselor. When I told her you wanted Leo, she started to cry.

While we waited for your mom, they moved us to a waiting room in the mental health ward. You kept saying that you didn't

Kristy and Leo, her favorite stuffed animal when she was little.
She asked for Leo again in the hospital.
July 1976 - Kristy at 5 years old.

understand why everyone was being so mean to you and why everyone was trying to ruin your life.

Later, as we were leaving, I remember you standing at the door holding Leo by his paw, looking like you were five years old. It was so very hard for your mom to leave you, but she didn't feel there was any choice.

APRIL 16
SHERRY

Kris had her first appointment with the psychiatrist this morning. My sister-in-law, Ann, took her, as I had to work. During the appointment, a nurse brought Kris out to the waiting room and told Ann they didn't feel it was safe for Kris to leave the hospital.

Ann called me to say I needed to come up to the hospital right away. Then she asked if Kris knew someone named Leo, as she was asking for him.

Leo is a stuffed animal, given by Kris' grandmother when she was five years old. It had been her favorite friend. As a child, she took Leo to bed with her every night and when she was a gymnast in high school, Leo went everywhere with the team as a mascot.

I am really scared: Why is she needing her childhood toy, a stuffed animal? What is happening?

When I saw Kris at the hospital, it was like seeing my five-year-old again. She grabbed Leo and hung on. The doctors told us we would have to leave Kris in that very scary place, that we could not stay with her.

I believed those doctors and trusted that they were smarter than me and would know what was best for my daughter. But I had deep misgivings as I looked at my daughter on the other side of the glass door. Tears were running down her face, which had a look that said she didn't understand what was happening or why she was being left there.

On my side of the door, tears were streaming down my face, too, as my heart was breaking. Oh my, what is happening and how can I leave her here alone? But I must leave so the doctors can help her get better. I need to be the strong one for Kris until they figure out what is wrong.

APRIL 16
KRIS

This was the day I checked into the psych ward at the hospital. My only memory is waking up one night and needing to use the bathroom, but the door to the restroom was locked. I tried to get the nurse's attention, but couldn't get anyone to unlock the door, so I ended up going to the bathroom on the floor next to the bed. I remember the nurses were frustrated.

Why is that the only memory I have of my eight days in the psych ward?

APRIL 16-23
SHERRY

This is my daughter. It is very hard to trust someone I don't know with the responsibility for her life.

This is indeed a very scary situation for me. I may have to leave Kris locked up on this floor with other mentally ill people. What might happen to her when she is alone and without any protection? All the scary things I have ever seen and heard about mental health institutions are running through my mind.

Nevertheless, that time of darkness
and despair will not go on forever.

Isaiah 9:1

Chapter 3

Blind Alley

APRIL 24
SHERRY

Nine days later and Kris is home with us.

I don't feel she is any better than when she checked into the hospital. In fact, if anything, Kris seems to be slipping further away from us.

This just is not making any sense. We have no answers, but where should we go? I need to figure out where to go for help but emotionally and mentally, I'm exhausted.

APRIL 25
SHERRY

Kris is not acting like the Kris I knew six months ago. She's really not her normal self, but who would be, after taking all of these drugs, especially when she doesn't usually even take aspirin?

The amount of medication alone is enough to make anyone act bizarre. But what I don't understand is how all these drugs can help when you mix so many together without testing each one separately to see how it might work. But her psychiatrist will not back down; he feels she needs all of these drugs.

So here is the plan set up by the psychiatrist: Kris will spend her mornings at the day hospital from nine until noon, working with the medical staff to figure out what is causing her confusion and disorientation.

I am still working and need my job, so either Ann or I will bring her to the hospital in the morning. At noon, her 82 year-old grandfather will drive into downtown St. Paul's busy traffic and pick her up. He will then stay with her at our house until 4:00 p.m., when either her dad or I return home from work.

We are afraid to leave her at home alone, even though she is 26 years old, because she has told us the dreams she has had about stabbing herself with our kitchen knives. No one can sleep for fear of what might happen.

When I come home from work and try to talk with Kris, she just stares at me without answering. She's is not happy about living with us and seems like she wants her independence, but we can't leave her alone.

How do I keep my sanity during this frightening time? My husband is always here to support and help, as well as our God, family and friends.

MAY 13
SHERRY

It has been a month since Kris came home from inpatient treatment. We've followed all of the psychiatrist's orders, yet nothing has improved and none of us feel we're closer to a solution.

When Roger and I met with the psychiatrist and nurses, we kept asking questions for which the psychiatrist didn't seem to have any answers.* At one point, he got up and started to walk out of the room, almost as if he was avoiding being put on the spot. We asked why he was leaving and his remark was, "I won't put Kris through your questioning about what is happening."

On the other hand, the nurses are encouraging us to continue asking questions. Like them, we feel that something else is wrong, but the psychiatrist doesn't seem to be very engaged.

What should we do?

*At that time, the Internet was not the huge information resource that it is today, so it was not easy to find the right doctor or research the information we needed.

I was sick and you looked after me.

Matthew 25:36

Chapter 4
Flight

May 15
SHERRY

My dad called me at work this afternoon. While he was doing some yard work at our house, Kris disappeared for a run and hadn't returned home yet. (You have to realize that Kris worships her grandfather and normally, would never just leave without the courtesy of telling him where she was going.)

Most of the time, my dad is a very calm person, but on the phone he sounded very afraid. He was talking fast and breathing hard. Now I needed to be concerned about him, too, as he has had a triple bypass and two stents; this situation is definitely too stressful for his heart. I had to go home right away, just to assure him that she was all right.

When I got home ten minutes later, Kris was standing in the kitchen with her hands and knees all bloody. She had this blank look on her face and said without any emotion, "I kept falling and couldn't get up."

This doesn't make any sense. What is going on now? What's next? I was very concerned, so I took her to the nearest doctor, who bandaged her hands and knees. When he asked how the injury had happened, we had no answers for him.

My gut tells me there might be a link between this accident and her illness, but I just don't know how to proceed.

After returning home from the clinic, a police officer rang our doorbell; he had followed a trail of blood to our house. A woman in the neighborhood had called the police to report that a young lady had fallen on the sidewalk and looked like she was having a seizure. (I just let that seizure part slide, as I couldn't imagine Kris having seizures.)

May 15
Kris

I remember being at my parent's house with Grandpa, but don't remember taking off for a run that day.

I do remember that, while I was running, I kept falling down and scraping my hands across the ground as I tried to get up. It was an indescribably odd sensation, accompanied by a tight, clenching feeling in my jaw.

I must have fallen down ten to fifteen times or more, but lost track while it was happening. I remember pushing my palms forward on the concrete sidewalk, but not being able to lift my hands, as if they weighed a thousand pounds each. It was like one of those dreams when you're trying to run but you can't move.

But it wasn't a dream and I didn't wake up.

Somehow, I made it home. I don't remember my Grandpa's reaction and was not in tune to how panicked he must have been.

I do vividly remember standing in the kitchen while he took care of me, lovingly putting wet paper towels on my hands and trying to comfort me. My mom came home shortly after that.

I sat there while this all unfolded, but had no feelings about what was happening. I was unemotional, detached and in a daze.

Pray continually...

1 Thessalonians 5:17

Chapter 5

Spiraling Down

JUNE 3
SHERRY

One night in early June, Kris became very upset and went to her room feeling quite angry with us. But she couldn't tell us why she was angry or what was wrong.

A couple of minutes later, Roger went into her room to find Kris' whole body shaking and convulsing. We had never seen anything quite like that before. We got her out of her bedroom and Roger kept her walking around to keep her awake while I called 9-1-1. We were concerned that she might have become over-medicated, as she was acting very strange and had no control of her body.

The Apple Valley police and paramedics came and took her vital signs and did the standard precautionary checks for drugs and paraphernalia. Then they took Kris by ambulance and we ended up in the emergency department of the hospital.

At 2:30 that morning, we took Kris home, as she refused to check into the psych ward again. She kept saying, "There is nothing wrong with me mentally." And we could not talk them into admitting her and intensifying the search for answers to her condition.

Looking back, I ask myself why we didn't go somewhere else. For one thing, when you're so emotionally tied up in a situation that threatens your child and you can't get solid answers, it's difficult to make any decisions.

For another, we were physically and mentally exhausted after three months of this and were having a hard enough time just keeping up with the day-to-day demands of our lives.

Besides, we kept thinking that tomorrow we would wake up and this would all disappear.

Bad things only happen to someone else, right?

Medical records entry: Kris is a twenty-six year-old female who was accompanied to the emergency department by her family. They state Kris appeared to be in a "fog" all throughout today and unwilling to talk to them. They state they were concerned that Kris may have had an overdose, as she seemed to be disoriented. Another concern was that she may have had a seizure. All medical tests came back negative and blood work showed she had not overdosed. She states she attends the day program here at the hospital and has an individual psychologist and psychiatrist. Kris did present as somewhat disoriented, however, was oriented to person, place and time and was able to state she is not suicidal and does not feel hospitalization will help her.

JUNE 10
SHERRY

I decided to stay home from work until I dropped Kris off at the day hospital at 9:00 a.m. Kris was having a hard time getting dressed, but finally we were on our way to the hospital, about 30 minutes from our house. We had arrived and were sitting in the parking lot when Kris got sick and lost her cookies. Now, most adults would move to avoid throwing up all over themselves, but she didn't seem to be aware of what was happening or able to clean herself up. I took her back home so she could change and clean up.

She said, "I can't go. I just need to rest for a couple of minutes." Kris laid down on the loveseat in our living room and seemed to fall asleep immediately. Meanwhile, the hospital called to see where she was; I said we would be back later if she felt better.

I remember rubbing Kris' temples and within minutes, they turned bright red. Then she began talking in her sleep. Kris seemed to be humming, talking in another language and seeing things all at the same time.

All of a sudden, Kris sat up, stared at nothing and said something incomprehensible. Then she fell back—all the while not recognizing that I was there with her. When I looked at her face and into her eyes, my heart curdled—where is our Kris? It was like someone else was controlling her. Have you ever seen "The Exorcist"? I was wondering if the devil was controlling Kris' mind and body.

I panicked. I was crying as I called Roger and told him I needed him RIGHT NOW! He came home in a half-hour, but it seemed like hours while I waited for his help. Again, we left for the hospital with Kris.

On the way, Kris was saying things that made no sense like, "There's a truck," and then look in another direction and say, "There's a bird." Her comments were totally illogical and incoherent, as she was not responding to her surroundings. Her comments were followed by maniacal laughter that sent chills down my spine.

When we got to the emergency room at the hospital, they took a CT scan of Kris' head and decided she needed to be admitted to the psych ward. Kris refused, so we took her home yet another time.

What are we to do? We are sure this is more of the same illness, but I'm afraid of what they will find and how long it will take them to help our daughter.

We still have no answers and don't know who to ask for help. *Where are you God? We need you.* Every night and day we pray, but no answers.

Come quickly to help me,
my Lord and my Savior.

Psalm 38:22

Chapter 6

Dark Passageways

JUNE 11
SHERRY

For the third time in ten days we brought Kris to the emergency room.

All of this is happening during one of my busiest weeks at school, but it is so frightening I can't even think about work. I have begun to realize that work is work, but family and God are the most important. All we can do is just survive each day.

Kris finally gave in. She had repeatedly refused to go to the psych ward, but today I wouldn't let her come home. Good thing, too, because on our way up to the psych ward, she had three *grand mal* seizures. The first lasted about 75 seconds and the next two lasted about two minutes each. I never realized how long two minutes could be until I watched my daughter having these seizures.

I should have recognized them as seizures, but when they first happened, I didn't know what to think. Was this part of some psychosis or was there something physically wrong?

At this point, I was just trying to hold on and not panic when her body lost control.

One of the nurses who was taking Kris from the emergency room to the psych ward questioned why we were going there saying, "Seizures are a sign of a more serious physical problem."

Grand mal seizures are not a sign of a mental illness, so I don't understand why we have to be in the psych ward, but that is where they put Kris. They put a monitor on her to watch her actions more closely for three full days, but still couldn't figure out what was wrong.

The second night in the mental health unit, a young male nurse was in charge of taking care of Kris. Roger told him to call if he had any problems. He assured Roger that he was strong and could handle Kris but he ended up calling Roger later that evening as he could not keep Kris in bed. Roger left home immediately and helped restrain and calm Kris down. Roger ended up spending most of the night there.

Medical records entry: Client experienced numerous mood swings, at times the patient was catatonic/defiant; and other times displayed inappropriate laughter; very sensitive to sounds which distract her easily; examines the room in fear; numerous reminders to not pull at the electrodes, seemed to forget the reasons why she should not do things. No long-term memory, is remembering family history; needs help remembering new information; disoriented, use of nonsense statements. Doctor ordered a spinal tap.

Hospital records entry: Client was admitted tonight and during the pre-interview, the client vomited and then in a three-hour period *experience three grand mal seizures; now compliant with EEG test. Disoriented and delusional; aggressive in rejection of EEG*; Anxious and experiencing panic attacks. Flat affect, delayed responding when addressed. Would not wear arm identification bracelet.*

*EEG (electroencephalogram) is a test used to detect abnormalities related to electrical activity of the brain.

JUNE 13
SHERRY

Finally, some relief. Today, they moved Kris out of the psych ward and into the neurological unit. Finally, I felt they would give us some answers. Little did I know how long we would wait.

They placed Kris in a private room, which would be her home for the next two months. I will always be able to picture that room in my mind: how can you ever forget the place where you fear your daughter might draw her last breath?

Her room is in a secluded part of the hospital, on an upper floor, at the end of a long hallway and through a double door. It feels like we're at the other end of the world and I won't be able to bring Kris back out.

The only way I can communicate with Roger is by leaving a message for him to call me back, as cell phones cannot be used in the hospital.

The medical team ran several tests, including a spinal tap. Based on the type of seizures Kris has had and the test results, they determined that the right side of her brain was slowing down. She had had intermittent bouts of agitation, but could still answer some simple questions.

To give you an idea of what Kris is going through: she has about twenty wires attached to her head so the medical staff can monitor her brain activity at all times. To attach these wires (which Kris is constantly knocking out) the nurse rubs Kris' head hard in a circular motion and then corkscrews the wires into her scalp. All the while, Kris squirms and whimpers in pain. I can barely watch.

I don't understand all of this, but I'm too afraid to ask many questions for fear I won't want to hear their answers. Most of the time, I just pray that Kris will keep fighting to breathe and survive. I keep asking God to keep her close to His heart.

How I plead with God,
how I implore His mercy,
pouring out my troubles before Him.
For I am overwhelmed and
desperate, and You alone know
which way I ought to turn.

Psalm 142:1-3

Chapter 7

Bleak Tunnel

JUNE 13-18
SHERRY

June 13th began with a neurologist's examination, but no answers. By the end of the day, Kris couldn't speak any more. *Oh please God, help us*, is all I can think and pray for.

During Kris' first four days in the neuro unit, I stayed overnight to watch over her. I slept on a cot in her room, although I never really relaxed enough to sleep.

I am too afraid to go home for fear Kris will leave me for God's world while I'm away.

On June 16th, Roger said he needed me to go home with him that night. Diane, the nurse on duty most nights, said she would keep a close eye on Kris and call us if there were any changes. At this stage, Kris is tied down by her arms and legs and sometimes even around her waist.

Hospital records entry: By June 16th the patient had lost speech and there was no verbal interaction. On June 16th Social Service involvement took place.

Medical records entry: Psychotic behavior. Patient did not respond verbally to parents or staff this a.m. Pulling at electrodes for EEG and needed constant monitoring or restraining of hands. While sitting in a chair, patient made strange formations with hands and two times appeared to have a visual hallucination and became fearful. At around 10 a.m. father told Kris he was going to leave and would be back later in the afternoon. Kris became upset. Seizure like activity – patient turned head to right, arched her neck, eyes rolled back and she was unresponsive. Later had clenched fists, rigid arm and tonic movements of legs and trunk of body. Hysterical laughing, patient salivating, and reddened face. Patient had 5 seizures throughout the day.

JUNE 17

At 12:30 a.m., Kris was fighting to get out of her bed. Staff had to restrain her hands to keep her safe and give her some medication to help her relax.

About 2:00 a.m., she was awake again and laughed uncontrollably for about 15 minutes. She had another laughing episode at 7:30 a.m. and then the neurologist decided they needed to do some nerve-end testing.

When I arrived at the hospital, the nurse told me it had taken six men to restrain Kris from leaving her bed last night.

We wonder what is going on in her head and why she is fighting to leave. She is physically strong, but mentally she can't communicate with anyone anymore. It's like trying to help an infant. Does she understand what is happening to her? Is she in pain? Is she as frightened as I am?

Every night, one of the family stayed with Kris until she fell asleep. She whimpered like a baby if she was awake when we left her room. Many nights and days we tried to comfort her by lying in her bed and holding her.

Why can't anybody find an answer? It is so frightening not to know what you are fighting against, but fight we do. Praying is part of our lives; it gives us great comfort and keeps our daughter alive.

God has many lessons for us to learn in life. My lesson is to be a gracious receiver, something that does not come easy for me. I am comfortable being the giver, but not the receiver.

Around this time, I had to accept a great many gifts. My co-workers offered to make meals and deliver them to our home. Because I didn't want to give up any of my time with Kris, I didn't feel I could be home to receive or organize the food. So, two very dear friends of mine, Lana and Sharon, organized the food and made all the arrangements. The food and my dear friends' help were greatly appreciated.

During this same time, two neighbors decided to take care of our yard, so my flowers were watered and our lawn was mowed. We also never worried about any bills. Ann—who was pregnant at the time—offered to take that task off my hands. "I can't do much physically, but I can manage Kris' account and make sure all the medical bills are paid."

This was a labor of love, as the thought of doing it made me sick to my stomach. These gifts from all these special people enabled me to spend my time focusing on my daughter.

On June 18, they started physical therapy. The therapists moved Kris' arms and legs while she was lying in bed.

Kris was very upset today. Several times, her whole body showed the agitation with jerky movements. She didn't seem to be able to relax and it was exhausting watching her being so upset. She was humming and crying, even in her sleep.

On June 19, the doctors did another spinal tap. Watching the procedure was so hard because I could see it was painful for Kris. They laid her on her stomach and then inserted a needle into her lower back; we tried to hold her still and help her not to move or cry out.

Later that day, they began to administer the antibiotics through an IV in her arm. Now why the antibiotics? I just can't keep up with understanding everything they are doing and sometimes, I just don't want to know.

On Friday, June 20th, Kris' face became blotchy. She became quite agitated again and then had dry heaves. Her blood pressure today is 122/90. They have been taking blood samples from Kris two to three times daily.

At 7:00 p.m., Dr. Penovich is still here, helping us with Kris. I wonder if she has a family. I will never forget this woman's endless compassion and love for my daughter.

Now I know why a nurse told me we were lucky that Dr. Penovich was on call when we first arrived at the hospital. I also know why the hospital felt it was quite a coup to have recruited Dr. Penovich from a hospital out East.

Never again will I ask why they become doctors—I know it is a very special calling that only a few are given. This I know: Dr. Penovich has been sent to us by God. She always goes the extra mile and is very supportive of our family. She even contacted some of the top neurology hospitals in the nation, including the Cleveland Clinic, for help with Kris' care.

JUNE 21-22

A different neurologist is on staff each weekend, so Kris has had several doctors by this time. This weekend, when Dr. Penovich was not on duty, another neurologist was sure he had found the answer. But by Monday, after Dr. Penovich had returned, we were apprised this was not the case.

JUNE 23

Most of Kris' veins have collapsed, making it impossible to draw blood for testing. So the doctors will place a catheter in her chest. This will mean putting her under general anesthesia. Will she be strong enough to wake up after the anesthesia? They decide there is no choice and go ahead with the procedure.

Another prayer is answered and the surgery is successful. Now that she has the catheter, it seems she is less agitated every time they take blood, which happens more frequently every day.

Hospital records state - Physical therapy was started on June 18th. On June 23rd a triple lumen catheter was placed by anesthesia for venous access, as laboratory draws were becoming very difficult.

I have told you all this so that
you may have peace in me.
Here on earth, you will have many
trials and sorrows. But take heart,
because I have overcome the world.

John 16:33

Chapter 8

Hanging By a Thread

Toward the end of June, while Dr. Penovich was out of the country, the head of the Neurology Department recommended that Kris have a brain biopsy of the right frontal lobe. He recommended a surgeon and surgery was scheduled for June 24th at 8:00 p.m.

A brain biopsy is the last resort, the last hope for a diagnosis after all other possibilities have been exhausted. In Kris' weakened state, the biopsy could cause seizures, strokes or a coma. She could die during the operation.

My friend, Lana, said it was important to have a list of questions for the doctor who is going to do the surgery. So I came with my list of questions such as, "How many surgeries like this have you done? How many surgeries have been successful?" and, "If you have been doing surgery all day, how will you have the energy to do Kris' surgery at 8:00 p.m.?" My final question was, "Are you a good doctor?" He smiled at Roger and me and said all surgeons are egotistical and he was very competent.

Then he said he would be shaving off all of Kris' hair. So this stubborn mom said, "Why do you need to remove all of her hair?"

His response was, "I need to make sure the area is sterile."

My comeback was, "I thought you said you were great and there wouldn't be any problems. And, if she lives, she will shoot me for allowing you to remove all her hair if it isn't necessary!"

Well, I won that battle; they only shaved off one square inch. But will Kris survive and ever realize how I fought to keep her hair?

During all of this, people I don't even know supported us and prayed for us. Our friends and family were always there. Our support system made all the difference, as someone was always helping us get through one more day.

Every night when we came home, we read the note pad on the kitchen counter on which Kris had written, "Kris loves Mom and Dad."

For some reason, I had saved that note instead of throwing it away. How many times did I read that note and wonder if Kris would ever be able to write me a note again? But it also gave me the courage to face another day.

Hospital records state – Since her clinical course had worsened (she was virtually mute, frequently agitated and restless), and laboratory data was essentially unremarkable, we held a discussion with Ms. Shuss' parents. The need for a right frontal brain biopsy was discussed. On June 25, a right frontal brain biopsy was obtained.

Feb 6, 1997

KRIS ♡'s
MOM and
Dad !

Mom ♡s Kris

Kris ♡'s Dad & MOM

DAD Love s Kris
BOPA

Our daily reminder that Kris was still with us.

JUNE 24

The day before the biopsy, the doctor told us that Kris would probably be in intensive care overnight and then back on the neurological floor the next day. She ended up being in intensive care for over a week; it became a very long week for me. Usually, someone was with me during those long days, but that week, both Lana and Sharon were out of town. I knew Roger had to be at work, but I hated being there alone.

It is amazing how much we value and depend on friends and family to help overcome problems. During Kris' illness, I really learned to accept help and depend on many people. That was not easy for me, as I would rather be the helper than the one who is helped.

JUNE 25

Brain biopsy occurred at 8 p.m. and morphine was ordered for pain as needed. The surgeon came out and said, "Everything went fine; the biopsy is being flown to the Mayo Clinic tonight."

We listened to the helicopter take off and cried.

JUNE 26

The day after the biopsy was rough for Kris. Every time they tried to remove the ventilator, her heart rate went up and she struggled to breathe. The nurses and neurologist asked Kris a question and she answered twice, "Yes, yes." She was unable to move her hands when they asked her, but when they asked her to move her feet, she was able to do that.

JUNE 27

Two days after the biopsy, Kris was running a temperature and the breathing problems returned. Because of the respiratory issues, they did an electrocardiogram (EKG) to test her heart rate and rhythm. The test results showed that her heart was slowing.

What does this mean? I'm not sure and am too scared to ask questions. Maybe if I don't hear any bad news, it won't become a reality.

Kris' has had several different medical staff in to evaluate her today; they are documenting her changes every hour. She is very lethargic and not moving towards improvement.

JUNE 28

Three days after the biopsy, Kris' heart stopped for seven seconds.

I need to pray harder and more.

Roger and I start to talk about Kris, but both of us are too afraid to continue. Neither of us wants to say our fears out loud for fear they will come true. We are both physically sick about what is happening.

*The Lord is my shepherd, I shall
not be in want...Even though I walk
through the valley of the shadow of
death, I will fear no evil, for you are
with me; your rod and your staff,
they comfort me.*

Psalms 23:1-4

A New Prayer

I go to the chapel in the hospital every day; there is no set time. I go when it is convenient to leave Kris or when I just can't handle it anymore and need some comfort, as it is one place I can find peace.

I go to pray and read the 23rd Psalm which is written on the wall behind the altar. I go to ask God to give me strength and to help Kris get well.

Today, my prayer was different. Instead of asking God to make Kris well, I prayed, "Okay, God, you have the control. If it is your will to take my daughter, you can take her. But, if for some reason, you think I need her more, please make her well for me."

After praying, I felt an immediate weight off my shoulders. I knew that God was in charge and all I needed to do was accept His comfort. The relief I felt is something I will never forget. God filled my heart and soul and I no longer needed to worry.

SUNDAY, JUNE 29
SHERRY

Four days after the biopsy, Kris is very quiet and lethargic during the day. This is not a good sign, but I cannot admit to myself that Kris might not make it.

JUNE 30
THE PACEMAKER

Kris was given 17 drugs today. So how can they tell how she's doing?

A neurologist and one of the cardiologists discussed putting a pacemaker in Kris to keep her heart beating. They are concerned that her blood pressure is 217/110, the heart monitor shows her heart is not in the correct rhythm and there have been times when her heart has stopped for a millisecond. They are concerned that it will stop and not start again.

It was decided they would install the pacemaker on July 1st, when they expected Kris to be strong enough and without any signs of infection.

Hospital records state – Post operatively in the ICU she had exaggerated vagal response during attempts to wean her off the ventilator. She had intermittent temperature elevations from 101.6 to 102 and consultation with infectious disease was also obtained.

*A vagal response is a reflex of the involuntary nervous system that causes the heart to slow down and affects the blood pressure.

The infectious disease specialist came down to see Kris in intensive care. He had seen Kris several times before, as he is the doctor who prescribed all the antibiotics.

Through all of this, I could sense when a doctor had a very deep feeling for my child. Maybe I should say there are some doctors I trusted more than others and some who seemed to go the extra mile.

The infectious disease specialist was the kind of doctor who made me feel I could ask any questions I had. He had already talked to us about our faith and I knew he had children, so I asked him, "If this was your daughter and they wanted to put a pacemaker in her, would you go for it?" I told him I was not just asking his professional opinion, but as one parent to another. He told me he would not sign the papers for Kris to have surgery the next day. By saying that, he gave me some time to think it through.

During Kris' first few days in intensive care, it was evident she was going to need someone to make medical decisions for her. Ann brought an attorney friend of hers into Kris' private room to talk to Kris about giving me power of attorney. This was a difficult and necessary decision to make, as Kris was not speaking or responding at that time.

The attorney turned to Kris and asked, "Is it okay if we give your mother the power of attorney?" Kris blinked. Then the attorney turned to me and asked, "If Kris blinks, does that mean she is saying yes?" I nodded.

The attorney signed the papers to give me power of attorney. She probably shouldn't have, but said she had a daughter and hoped someone would do this for her if it were ever necessary.

The love of all kinds of people comes out at times like this. She left, saying she would be praying for us. And we needed everyone's prayers.

JULY 1

The cardiologist still thinks that a pacemaker is the appropriate choice, but Kris still has a low-grade temperature. I bounced back and forth all day between options, trying to make a decision. By the end of the day, I decided I would not sign for the pacemaker unless Roger wanted it.

No parent should have to make these life-and-death decisions for their child. All these choices—which are the right ones for her health?

After Roger and I spent an hour watching a film on pacemakers that covered everything that could happen during the surgery, we opted not to have it done. Our gut feeling was that Kris had gone through so much pain and stress already that another invasive surgery would be too hard on her. Not to mention that a pacemaker isn't removed when it's no longer needed; it would be in there for the rest of her life.

Over the next few days, as Kris' heart started to beat more regularly, it became unnecessary for Kris to have the pacemaker. After all the agonizing, the weight was lifted off my shoulders. Thank God I did not have to make this life-changing decision for my daughter.

Meanwhile, flowers and cards were pouring in from all over. A sister-in-law in Ohio heard of a shrine to Our Lady of Toledo.

She drove there to request special prayers for Kris and to bring back holy water. Now, this may not seem like anything special, but this sister-in-law would never drive there under normal circumstances, as she is afraid to drive in heavy traffic. It is amazing how you can overcome your fears to help someone else.

Kris also received a cloth that had been touched and prayed over by every member of a church, none of whom knew Kris. Sister Ann from St. Joe's in Rosemount came and prayed with us for Kris, as did the Archbishop from Northfield. Another person gave us a card that said, "Believe in Miracles." Yet another friend had a medal blessed in Medjugorje, a town in the Herzegovina region of Bosnia where apparitions of the Virgin Mary have appeared since 1981.

I can still remember one day in the latter part of June when three of Kris' friends phoned on the same day. They must have all sensed we needed them. Tifani called from Vienna, Denise called from her office in Minneapolis and Janna called from Florida. Basically, all three told us to keep the faith, as Kris would get better.

How we held onto these positive messages that gave us hope!

Be strong and courageous,
for your LORD your God goes with you;
he will never leave you nor forsake you.

Deuteronomy 31:16

Chapter 9

The Vortex

JULY 2

Kris is not eating. She continues to lose weight—she's less than 100 pounds now, so they decide to place a feeding tube into her stomach. She also has a bladder infection, so the catheter will have to be removed.

Today, Kris walked twice. Physical therapy is working with her to relearn how to sit and stand but, without assistance, her knees buckle and she falls.

I am scared every single time the staff takes her for a walk, because they first have to disconnect every lead on her head from the brain monitor. This means her brain activity is not monitored during those walks and the medical staff could miss something critical. She is still in intensive care and her health is so fragile, it makes me very nervous.

This afternoon, Kris' heart rate jumped to 149 when she saw me packing up her things to move her out of intensive care and back to her regular room in the neurology department. She had tremors and sat up in a rigid position for a half-hour. Nurse Shelly and I gave her a bath, but the agitation continued for hours. Finally, she settled down about 3 p.m., only to resume the agitation a couple of hours later. This evening, her temperature bumped up to 101.3.

The head of neurology called and set up a conference for tomorrow to review the biopsy results we have been waiting for. A swallowing study is also scheduled for tomorrow.

What a full day! No wonder I never seem to have the time to evaluate *what* we are doing versus what we *should* be doing. It seems like all I do is react to what is happening.

JULY 3
DIAGNOSIS OR DEATH SENTENCE?

Today, we met to discuss the biopsy findings. Our conference included the social worker, psychiatrist, nurses, the neurologist, Roger and me. Dr. Penovich, my rock, is out of the country, so the head of neurology met with us instead.

The doctor delivered his diagnosis as tepidly as a weather report. "Kris has vasculitis.* She will probably never leave a nursing home, as she will be both mentally and physically handicapped for the rest of her life. She will not be able to talk or take care of her basic needs; she will live in a diaper."

I started to interrupt him and he said, "Just wait until I finish."

Vasculitis is an inflammation of the blood vessels in the brain. Central nervous system vasculitis can affect both the brain and the spine and often occurs with viral or bacterial infections and autoimmune diseases. At the time of Kris' illness, vasculitis was an extremely rare, deadly disease.

I don't remember if he said anything else noteworthy because I simply blanked out. You see, the doctors have given us a different diagnosis almost every week since Kris was first examined. We've heard so many theories and possibilities, but none have solved the mystery of Kris' illness.

And now he tells me my daughter is going to die, after all. How long have they been trying to tell me that Kris' illness could be terminal? I don't know, but this was the first time I heard them.

At this moment, the psychiatrist says, "Excuse me. I have to leave for another appointment." The doctor delivers Kris' death sentence and the psychiatrist has something more important to do?

The doctor looked at me and said, "Mom, you look like you have something to say." Everyone knows that I have plenty to say, and say it I did.

"Well, doctor, you don't know my family nor do you have our faith. When Kris was born, a doctor told me she would probably have brain damage and many other problems. Well, he was wrong and so are you. We will do whatever is necessary to get her better. Fight we will. Pray we will."

They will treat the vasculitis with 80 milligrams of steroids for two days and then a reduced amount for two weeks.

The next challenge to face today is surgery. They have no choice but to surgically insert a feeding tube so Kris can receive nutrition and medication. After surgery, they will place Kris in a bed with a built-in scale so they know how much food to put through the tube. She is running a temp between 101 and 102.

Once again, Kris will be under general anesthesia. Once again, I worry if she will wake up.

Medical records entry: On July 3, a care conference was held with Ms. Shuss's parents, the social worker, neurologists, psychiatrists, and staff from Station 7900. We reviewed her cardiac status and preliminary pathology report from the Mayo Clinic which ruled out Jakob-Creutzfeldt's disease and Rasmussen's encephalitis. The likely preliminary pathology diagnosis was encephalopathy secondary to vasculitis.* EEG showed diffuse slowing. She was exhibiting brainstem release findings, such as chewing movements along with tremors and posturing.

With Pathology reporting possible vasculitis, education regarding this was given to all. We informed them that her clinical status could worsen over the next few months. We discussed the use of steroids with a frank discussion regarding risk of infection, bleeding and death. On July 3, a PEG** tube was surgically placed by a doctor for nutritional needs.

*Percutaneous Endoscopic Gastronomy - a feeding tube.

JULY 4

When we called the hospital this morning, Kris' temperature was up to 103. The doctors were so concerned that we called a family meeting. Mark and Robin, my brother and his wife, brought my parents to their home. On our way there, we stopped to get donuts—like we needed to do that.

We all tried explaining to my parents that they must see Kris today. My mom, at the age of seventy-four, wasn't having a "good day." She kept saying, "We'll come tomorrow; today's not good." Finally, they realized what we were telling them: the doctor was saying, *Come today, there might not be a tomorrow.* So we all went to the hospital. Seeing Kris was extremely difficult for them, as they are very close; I watched my parents age right in front of me.

After Kris' grandparents left, because of Kris' rapid decline they did another spinal tap and put her back on antibiotics.

That evening, when Roger and I walked out to the parking lot, we held each other and cried while we watched the fireworks from the hospital. Would we ever watch the fireworks again with our daughter? Now, every year on the 4th of July, I get this lump in my throat. I thank God and I wonder why there is so much suffering in the world.

Medical records entry: A third lumbar puncture revealed WBC's (white blood cells). *

*WBCs, also called leukocytes or leucocytes, are the cells of the immune system that are involved in protecting the body against both infectious disease and foreign invaders. The number of leukocytes in the blood is often an indicator of disease.

JULY 5

The physical therapists work with Kris almost every day. It is essential that they keep her moving because her muscles (including her heart muscle) will atrophy and the movement helps to flush the drugs from her system.

Kris' temperature was high in the morning, but improved in

the evening. Then, just when we thought things were getting better, she regressed and had an hour-long episode where she stiffened up like a board, clenched her jaw, gritted her teeth, shook and become very fearful of anyone who got close to her. She couldn't sit still, track people or even see anyone.

Later in the afternoon, Kris had lots of company besides Roger and me. Brad, Ann and Josh stopped by. Kris was not up to walking today, so we put her in a wheelchair and took her down the street to the Dairy Queen.

Most of the time when we talk with her, Kris doesn't react, as if she doesn't understand anything we say. But today, when we offered her a spoonful of ice cream, she opened her mouth! You could not imagine everyone's surprise, as this was the first time in a couple of weeks that Kris voluntarily opened her mouth to take in any food.

Is this a gentle whisper from God letting us know He is there, to hang onto our hope?

About 8:30 p.m. she quieted down, but at 8:45 another episode began. She also seemed to panic when anyone moved fast, and was salivating with bubbles. What is happening?

JULY 6
SUNDAY

I checked in with Polly, her nurse, as we are going to church before coming up to the hospital. She said Kris was having a good morning and seemed to be tracking everyone who came into her room.

Every Sunday when we go to church, I look at the verse above the altar, "Come to me all who are burdened and I will refresh you." I keep thinking and asking God, "When does this refreshment come?"

After we got to the hospital, Kris had a couple more episodes of agitation. She has to be medicated for these episodes because she is so aggressive and strong that they can't always control her. They have to tie her to her bed by the wrists, ankles and even around the waist.

Most of the afternoon, Kris just lay in her bed with her eyes open, trance-like, not connecting with anyone through eye contact or words. She was very lethargic again.

JULY 7

Shelly is back from vacation, so I know things will go better today. This is the nurse who has spent many days and nights taking care of Kris, often working double shifts despite the fact that she is newly married. Shelly is only 25 (one year younger than Kris). Shelly is one of Kris' guardian angels.

Despite how unresponsive Kris might be on any given day, Shelly still treats her with great dignity, respect and understanding. While most hospital patients wear gowns, Shelly makes a point to shower and dress Kris every day. She puts Kris into a wheelchair and rolls her into the shower. Then she supports Kris' head and body during the shower. More often than not, Shelly gets a shower too.

JULY 8

Kris began the day quite upset. After they gave her a cocktail of anti-anxiety, anti-psychotic and anti-spasmodic medications she was able to relax the rest of the morning. She was talking some and actually answered the doctor with yes or no.

She has had lots of company, but gets very frustrated trying to talk with them because she is not able to find the right words or to clearly express herself. Much of the time, she doesn't seem to know what is happening, but during her lucid times, I can see pain in her eyes and in her body language. It was a tough night trying to get her calmed down enough to sleep.

Medical record entry: Kris began opening her eyes somewhat and could walk for longer periods. She appeared to have increased dystonia along with frank hallucinations. Ativan, Cogentin and Navane were given. She had not been sleeping well prior to this. The following day she was awake and was vocalizing nonsensical speech. Later that day, speech again disappeared.

JULY 9

Kris didn't seem to be able to talk today. She slept a lot. They are going to put the catheter back in, so we decided we'd try to get her to use the bathroom. Unsuccessful there, we next tried the portable and then finally gave up and helped Kris get back into bed. So then the urge came and she urinated on the bed.

We and the staff were so happy to see Kris relax and urinate; another step towards recovery.

JULY 10

This see-sawing back and forth is so frustrating. Today, she did very little talking and didn't make eye contact. But she did walk. Kris also had her third MRI.

Shelly is concerned that Kris is still losing weight, even with the feeding tube, so she spends a lot of time feeding Kris with a syringe to ensure she gets more calories and nutrition. She syringes the food into the back of Kris' mouth and then massages her throat to get the food to go down.

Robin brought Ryan and Jake to see Kris. Before today, Jake (who is eight and very tender-hearted) was scared to come to the hospital. It's not easy for an eight-year-old to understand what is happening to his cousin.

But his ten-year-old brother, Ryan, was able to visit Kris and had the wisdom of an adult. He showed such love to Kris. I watched him for twenty minutes as he fed Kris with the syringe and rubbed her throat. Then her friend, Tifani, showed up to visit her in the evening.

Medical records entry: A high dose of cortisone was started.

JULY 11

By 9 a.m., Shelly had Kris up, showered, her hair in a French braid and walking. Then she had Kris eating yogurt and drinking juice. At lunch, Kris ate applesauce and chocolate pudding.

The physical therapist came and had Kris walking out in the hallway all the way to the windows outside of the station. Kris came back exhausted and slept for four hours. When she woke up, she lost her cookies and had another episode of tremors and agitation. It seems like we take two steps forward and three steps back in the same day.

Medical records entry: She has very rare words. Walking was better.

JULY 12

For Kris, walking down the hospital corridor is like an ordinary person climbing Mount Everest.

At first, Kris couldn't put one foot in front of the other or even stand up, because her body was so very rigid. Shelly worked many hours, over many days to help Kris walk.

When Kris goes for a walk down the hallway, at least four people walk with her. There is a person holding her on each side, someone walking behind her (at times, this person has to push Kris into a standing position) and then someone in front encouraging Kris to walk forward, like you would with a baby who is learning to walk.

Going outside is a production too—we always need at least two people and a wheelchair. We need two people because we never know how Kris is going to react. And we need the wheelchair because we never know when Kris will get too tired and just sit down wherever she stops.

JULY 13

There doesn't seem to be any consistent pattern to the good days and the bad days. Today, Kris is smiling. We haven't seen her smile in so long we almost forgot what it looked like. She looks happy, but we really don't know what she is thinking,

Before the illness with cousins and grandparents.
L to R, Grandma Marie, my cousin Jake, the "tender-hearted one,"
Ryan, the one "with the wisdom of an adult," Josh, the "one who sang
me lullabies," me (Kris Shuss Kelbrants, holding Josh) and behind us,
Grandpa Archie Mikiska, "the rock" of the Mikiska family.

as she is unable to share that with us.

Most evenings, Kris is agitated and inconsolable. Tonight, she had hallucinations and tremors for about a half-hour. It was so frightening. After these episodes, it's hard to settle her down so she can relax and go to sleep. Her temperature is up to 100 degrees again.

On many nights like these, Kris' uncle, Brad, and his two-year-old son, Josh, would come to the hospital and sing lullabies to help Kris relax and fall asleep.

JULY 14

Another frightening day. Kris hallucinated for about 45 minutes and her blood pressure jumped to 182/118, so they put the brain monitor wires back on her head again. At noon, she had another episode of posturing, so they gave her some Navitol to help her. Meanwhile her temperature climbed to 101 degrees, so at 3 p.m. they gave her some Tylenol and decided she needed intravenous antibiotics.

This is another day when I don't know if this illness is going to take our daughter or not.

Medical records entry: She continued to have posturing and tremors. She had periodic bouts with increase in heart rate and elevated blood pressure. Cardiology consultation was re-obtained to evaluate the need for a beta blocker for autonomic overdrive. Temperatures at that time continued to vacillate, elevating up to 101.6.

An internal medicine doctor was consulted regarding the need for possible anti-hypertensive medication. This was considered, but never initiated. Her bouts of increased agitation with elevated heart rate and blood pressure lessened.

JULY 15

Today, Kris walked for the first time without us holding her up. We walked outside, down to the children's garden and then back again.

But later, she had three bouts of posturing and tremors that lasted about 45 minutes each. During these episodes, it didn't seem like Kris was inside her body.

When I say posturing, I mean that her whole body stiffens like a board. She doesn't move and simply stares. During an episode, she can't communicate with anyone; she doesn't even seem to be aware of what is happening to her, like she's in a trance.

This afternoon, I met with Social Services and talked about us finding a facility for Kris after she is discharged from the hospital. I also need to consider where she can go based on who will accept her and how we will pay for this. Kris does not have short-term disability insurance because she voluntarily quit her job. I'm not sure where to begin, who to ask or how to do any of this. And how do I think about all of this when all my energy needs to be focused on praying to keep Kris alive?

This evening, Kris' upper body, arms, back and shoulders stiffened up. She finally settled down at 9:15 p.m.

Ĵᴜʟʏ 16

Exhausted by the recent posturing episodes, tremors and hallucinations, Kris slept in this morning. After waking up, Kris took a walk, ate lunch and then napped. When Tifani came to visit, we took Kris on another walk. While Shelly and I were helping Kris walk this afternoon, she fell sound asleep standing up!

The doctors decided to take Kris off Navane and try something new.

Medical records entry: Navane was discontinued and Haldol was started.

Fighting for Faith

Our battle to have faith for Kris' healing was challenged constantly. While the doctors and medical staff were sympathetic, they cautioned us not to get our hopes up. So we fought daily to be positive, keep our faith strong and remain hopeful while living under a dark cloud of medical authority.

This is why Roger and I insisted that there be no negativity in Kris' room. Discussions with the medical staff took place in the hall where Kris couldn't hear, in case something negative was said.

We were very protective of Kris' energy and time and kept the number of visitors to a minimum throughout her illness. We didn't want to share what could be our last moments with Kris with anyone but immediate family and our very closest friends.

JULY 17

Dr. Penovich is back in the country and in charge of Kris' care again. I have missed her greatly; I have such confidence in her knowledge and in her commitment to Kris getting well.

Dr. Penovich says they will decrease the steroids to 40 milligrams tomorrow and will increase her calorie intake, as she continues to lose weight. They also decided to take Kris off Cogentin and start her on another new drug tomorrow, as they feel it might be causing the problems with urination.

For some reason, today I called the Lupus Foundation to see if they had any suggestions. The lady who answered the phone said, "If you think your daughter has lupus, you need to see Dr. Ridley. He's the lupus expert. He's the best. He's the one you need to see." So I asked Dr. Penovich if she could contact Dr. Ridley to come and see Kris.

Medical records entry: Risperdal was started. Haldol and Navane were slowly discontinued. A physiatrist was consulted about possible rehab potential and input into long-term placement setting. Also consulted was Dr. Ridley for rheumatology.

JULY 18
FEAR

Kris' physical abilities are coming back, but will her mental abilities ever return? This is something I can't say out loud; I am so afraid to think, much less talk about, what skills and abilities Kris might lose permanently.

Every night, I pray that she will regain her intellect. Right now, the girl who graduated *cum laude* from college can't add 1+1.

Will the old Kris ever come back to us? We pray that the girl who smiled and laughed is still in there.

Kris went down to physical therapy and then her friend, Janna, stopped by to see her. She was not really focused on her surroundings and drooled a lot. Shelly had her walking some more but then Kris needed a catheter to empty her bladder. This afternoon she had more bouts of agitation and posturing.

It's been a week since the conference with the neurologist and Kris isn't getting better. We have to face facts: just because we have a solid diagnosis doesn't guarantee Kris is going to get better.

Tonight when she had a visitor, Kris reached out her hand. This is a good sign that the old Kris is still inside and, hopefully, will come back to us. It is especially important because it means she is, at times, aware when people come into her room and is able to recognize some of them.

Even though this only happens occasionally and for just a few brief moments, we choose to hold onto these good times.

July 19

Kris is very sleepy today. She's sitting in a chair staring straight ahead and not responding to her surroundings.

While I was reading, another doctor that I'd never met before came waltzing in, carrying Kris' large binder of medical records. He introduced himself as Dr. Ridley, opened Kris' file and started to explain Kris' condition. He was so matter-of-fact and confident in his delivery it made me feel like he did know. He explained that Kris "clearly has vasculitis" and described the treatment plan with such clarity and intention, my gut told me he was going to be able to help us.

Kris did well in physical therapy. She really hasn't been able to walk in a straight line unless we guide her. Every step has been stiff and jerky and she has bumped into objects in her path. Today, she was able to walk around them.

JULY 20

Brad and Ann brought Josh to visit today, Kris made eye contact and smiled at him. Not a big deal you say, but this was a glimpse of Kris before she became ill. Even if it was just for a couple of minutes, she wore her old smile that we all love.

Her dad told her he could use a hug and then, very slowly, reached for her and hugged her. (You never move quickly towards her, as that scares her.) When he moved back, she looked at him and smiled.

That smile lit up our world.

JULY 21
HOPE

I am listening to a song on the radio in her room, "How am I supposed to live without you?"

Life is such a struggle right now. I just keep asking God each day and praying for Him to give me strength to handle what is to come. I keep praying that Kris will come back to us—and I don't mean just physically. I miss her smile so much and the way it lights up her eyes. Will that ever happen again?

When just the two of us are in her room, I tell her how much I need the joy only she can bring to my life. I tell her that I know she is in there, fighting, and that I will keep fighting with her, no matter how long it takes us. I ask her to be strong and tell her if she thought gymnastics was tough, it was just a warm-up to this fight that she must win. I tell her she can do it, to keep her faith, pray to God and together, we will get there. I tell her that I know I'm asking a lot of her, but with God's help, she can do it.

Later today, she got out of bed by herself for the first time. Before today, she hadn't even tried.

JULY 22

Kris needed another spinal tap today. I hate having to watch her, as I know it is painful and she has been through so much pain already. I was just not up to handling it today and broke down in tears.

Dr. Penovich said she and Shelly would stay with Kris through the procedure. She said I just needed to breathe and get away from the hospital. I said, "I need to go pick out a care center."

Dr. Penovich put her arms around me and said, "Just go and rest. We won't make her leave the hospital until you are ready. I will delay her leaving. This is something we will do for you." She is such a caring doctor.

Some good news: the spinal tap results were better. The first time, her number was 30 and today it is 7. Normal is 1 or 2, but at least we are going in the right direction.

Medical records entry: Fourth lumbar puncture was obtained on July 22 which revealed a decrease to 7 WBC's. Between July 21 and July 25, Ms. Shuss became more responsive with more periods of alertness and visual tracking.

JULY 23

Kris walked for one and a half hours today and drove the physical therapy crew crazy. She wouldn't stop walking. Then she walked again with Janna and Dad. Later, Tifani came to the hospital and managed to get some smiles out of Kris.

Another first: Kris walked up 18 stairs, which she hasn't been able to manage before.

We took Kris to the chapel and prayed with her.

Today I started looking at care centers. Ann went with me. Finding a care center is something most people realize they may have to do for their parents—but not for their children.

I asked my list of questions and choked on doing this. Some places smelled. When I walked into some of the care centers, I felt like I was going to hell. I can't describe how horrible this made me feel.

Kris' friend Janna, a physical therapist, brought us a list of care centers to check out. She had highlighted ones that she thought would be best for Kris.

JULY 24

Shelly put in another long day—from 6:30 a.m. until 11:30 p.m.—to make things better for Kris. She is always there, working extra shifts, always encouraging and making things as normal as possible for Kris.

While doing paperwork at the support desk in the center of the unit, Shelly looked up and said, "Oh my God!" Kris was standing in the doorway looking and smiling at her.

While Shelly was feeding Kris, she wanted to get up and wouldn't continue eating. So finally, Shelly gave up on the meal and helped Kris get up and walk to the bathroom. She had difficulty persuading Kris to sit, but finally, Kris used the bathroom.

Next, Kris went to the physical therapist and walked again. She also tried using her hands today and seemed more alert.

Kris is not speaking, nor is she aware of what is happening around her most of the day. However, when Roger held out "Wrinkles," a plush toy dog, she tried reaching for it. And when Roger asked her to stick out her tongue, she did it. Not many people would consider this important, but we think every step is a giant step towards renewed health.

When evening came, we took several steps back—she had three seizures starting at 10 p.m.

Just when we think things are looking up, we get hit in the head with another reality check. Will this ever stop?

Medical records entry: By July 24, mentation began to markedly improve. She walked by herself with assistance of nursing staff. She had three generalized tonic-clonic seizures and Dilantin was added to her medication regime.

JULY 25

In response to the seizures yesterday, they started Kris on Dilantin and increased her steroids. Today, I visited more care centers, supported by my friend Sharon. Kris slept most of the day and evening with no tremors in her hands.

JULY 26

Kris is still very sleepy today. We went for a short walk and then took her for a ride outside in the wheelchair. There were no tremors of her hands again today. Grandpa came to visit with Kris for a couple of hours. There has always been a special relationship between the two of them.

Tonight, we ordered pizza for the staff and tried to have some laughs with them before we left for the care center.

JULY 27

Kris does not want to open her eyes this morning, even though she is not sleeping. Later in the morning, Roger and I took her for a walk. Roger told her that if she wanted to go outside, she would need to push the "DOWN" button on the elevator. He kept pointing to the button and repeating that she should push the button. Finally, she did it—another big step.

Later, we took her to the water fountain and asked her if she wanted to have a drink. He showed her how to turn on the water many times until she copied him. Her upper extremity movements are fairly well-controlled, so she was able to do these things.

Robin brought Ryan and Jake to visit Kris again. She really

checked them out, but still no talking. It is time to pick out a care center.

JULY 28

Kris had a good day again. This morning, she had more control of her walking, but then the afternoon came and walking became a challenge. She rubbed her face and eyes continuously today. What causes some of these behaviors and will they ever stop?

Medical records entry: By July 29 tremors had completely abated. More normally coordinated and purposeful movements occurred, such as reaching for her nose to itch it, reaching for crayons and writing utensils. She would get up and walk to the water fountain and press the button to drink. She was more visually attentive. EEG background improved. A conference was held with the mother, father, social worker, Dr. Penovich and nurse clinician. We discussed long-term options. They requested that her chart be copied in case they would like a second opinion on an outpatient basis. They were given names for referral at the University of Minnesota or Mayo Clinic.

JULY 29

Kris was moving more today and even did a little dance, swinging her butt and then squatting down. Tifani came and did her nails, but Kris is still not talking.

Shelly was trying to feed Kris with a syringe, but Kris kept backing away. So Shelly picked up the cup and handed it to Kris, who actually took it and set it on the tray. Prior to this, Kris has not had enough coordination to hold anything. Shelly kept telling Kris, "If you won't take the cup to eat and drink, I will have to feed you with the syringe."

Now, we don't know if she comprehended what was said, but Shelly wouldn't give up and Kris kept shaking her head, "No." Kris finally looked at her and said, "What are you doing?" as though she was a little irritated, and then popped back into her shell again.

I know we have to be patient, but everything takes so long to accomplish. We're exhausted.

Later in the day, Kris was walking outside and became enamored with the green grass. This was the first time she was aware of grass—she wanted to touch it and sit on it.

This is one of those little things that lets you know God is always with you. It is so easy in life to not appreciate the little things. Each day, I have a new understanding that just getting up in the morning is a miracle.

JULY 30

Today, we took Kris outside for another walk to the Dairy Queen where she took a couple of bites of ice cream. She was smiling again today.

While we were out, she walked up to a yellow Cadillac and was very curious about it. She walked around it and looked inside it too. When we returned to her room, she walked to the window and saw herself for the first time. She spent about ten minutes just checking out her own self. Then she went to bed and slept the rest of the day.

Dr. Ridley's notes state: Patient has isolated CNS Vasculitis – will increase prednisone to 40 mg. for 1 month to 6 weeks and then begin steroid taper. Only consider methotrexate or cytoxin if patient cannot tolerate taper.

JULY 31

Kris was curious about the phone and picked it up. So I called her cousin, Jake, and he talked with her. Kris didn't answer or acknowledge that she understood who was talking with her. We tried walking some more today and she seemed more alert.

AUGUST 1

Both Dr. Ridley and Dr. Penovich were very positive today because Kris is showing some great signs of improvement. She has been looking in the mirror after rolling up her sleeve and flexing her muscles. She also turned the light switch on and off several times and stared and waved at people in the physical therapy area.

The sun is out today and it is 80 degrees. I feel like the world is getting right, even though I noticed that my diamond fell out of my wedding ring somewhere in the hospital today. It is just a material thing.

Kris was quite agitated tonight and seemed like she was despondent or upset.

AUGUST 2

SHERRY

I'm at a breaking point. It's been two weeks since we got the diagnosis, but I'm not seeing her mental capabilities improving.

The fact is that Kris may never recover. I couldn't face it this morning, so Roger skipped golf and spent the morning and part of the afternoon with Kris.

Until now, Kris has spoken a few words, but without recognizing to whom she was speaking. She still panics and flinches if someone gets too close too quickly. So when I come in to see her, I am careful not to approach her too fast, as she frightens easily and jumps if there are any sudden movements.

So when I came to see her this afternoon, I knelt in front of her chair. I tried to make eye contact with her and said, "Kris, I would like to hug and kiss you."

She said, "Of course you can, Mom."

My tears started flowing because it was like she was normal again. After the rough morning I had had, this was a strong message from God that Kris was still "in there." It gave me the strength I needed to keep going.

All the nurses and the doctors came in and started checking all her vital signs, but nothing new showed up and she did not talk again that day.

This is a day to appreciate how fortunate we are to have God in our lives.

After Kris brushed her teeth, she smiled and seemed proud of herself. If you know Kris, she normally brushes her teeth at least three times a day. It makes sense that this would be one of the first habits that comes back to her.

We could hardly believe she got up and did the bathroom thing herself. Even I will be glad not to help her in the bathroom.

I'm so proud of Kris and how hard she is working to get better. Tonight, we had a long discussion with her, telling her how many people from different churches have been praying for her.

We are not sure whether she understands any of this or ever will.

AUGUST 3
SUNDAY - GOD'S DAY

Kris seems to get better and better every day. Today, she is quite upset about the PEG in her stomach. She keeps reaching for it, wanting to pull on it and we must pull her hands away.

Robin phoned this morning and I asked her to talk to Kris as if Kris is completely normal and understands everything. This is something I ask every family member to do when they speak with Kris. We didn't expect Kris to answer Robin, as she hadn't talked since yesterday.

But when Kris heard Robin's voice today, she said, "Robin, Robin, Robin, Mark busy." Didn't know what that meant, but this was the first time she recognized anyone's voice on the phone.

Robin was so excited she said they were coming right up to the hospital. When Robin and the boys arrived, Kris hugged Jake and cried, then she hugged Ryan and cried and then she hugged Robin and cried some more.

What blessings we have received.

The LORD will fight for you;
you need only to be still.

Exodus 14:14

Chapter 10

A Fork in the Road

AUGUST 4
SHERRY

Another day of big changes. Today, we are leaving the hospital and moving Kris to a care center. This move is scary, but we know Kris can't function at home with a feeding tube in her stomach and wearing diapers.

So we're taking her to live at Lake Ridge Care Center in Roseville—even further away than the hospital—but we all agreed this is the center that will be the best for Kris.

Kris was so jittery and easily spooked I was afraid she would try to get out of the car while we were driving to Lake Ridge. I knew I couldn't handle Kris on my own, so I asked Robin to ride with us. Robin and I sat in the back seat with Kris between us, just in case she tried to open the door and get out of the car. After all these precautions, Kris fell asleep almost as soon as we got in the car. So much for all that worrying!

When we got to the care center, Kris was given a room with an elderly lady. They assured us the arrangement would work just fine. About an hour later, Kris' random outbursts of laughing, crying and shouting convinced them she needed a private room.

Then they assured us we wouldn't need to stay, as the facility was locked and everyone needed to sign in and out. (Kris was given a wristband that would trigger the alarm on the door should she attempt to leave. The staff could accommodate the elderly, but not a 26-year-old who could run faster than any of them.) After another hour passed, they were encouraging us to stay in the room with her; they even brought a cot into the room for me.

It took them less than an hour to realize Kris needed twenty-four-hour supervision, as she was completely unpredictable and had no idea what was going on. One minute, she would be walking around in her diapers, connected by her feeding tube to the IV pole. The next minute, she would crash and sleep for hours.

I knew Kris could get quite agitated and I didn't know if I could control her or persuade her to stay in her room or in the care center. You could not sit her down in bed for five minutes and trust she would be there when you got back. She didn't know where she was or what she was doing so believe me, I was scared too! Would this work?

I just didn't know what to expect and didn't have any nurses to help me if I ran into a problem. The first night went quite well—Kris fell asleep quickly without too much agitation. I was exhausted and the peace and quiet was a gift.

AUGUST 5
DAY 2 AT THE CARE CENTER

Kris' room has two single beds, an attached bathroom, a TV with a video player (you will soon understand its importance) and a telephone.

Lake Ridge has a bird cage in the main lobby that Kris just loves to sit and watch. It also has an enclosed outdoor courtyard where I can take Kris and not worry she will run away. The courtyard has a garden and many tables and chairs for visiting with family and friends. That's where Kris feels most comfortable; she never wants to go into the dining room with the elderly people.

Kris woke up at 6:30 a.m. We managed to get her to the bathroom before she had an accident. Believe me, this was not an easy feat, as we have to manage the long "tail" of equipment so it doesn't get knocked over. Mission accomplished. Kris fell back asleep at 7:15, but was up and in the bathroom again at 7:45.

Kris has physical therapy at 11:00 a.m. She makes the therapists jog with her. Kris still has one speed—hard and fast—which most people can't keep up with.

My friend, Sharon, brought Kris a shirt from the Cheers pub in Boston. Later, when Kris was showing Roger, the shirt she said, "Cheers-cheers-cool."

She is starting to recognize more people and is sometimes able to associate people with their family members. For example, she saw a picture of Roger's brother and said, "Ron and Tyler," remembering that Tyler is one of Ron's sons.

Still, her physical ability is coming back much more quickly than her mental skills.

AUGUST 6

Kris went for a walk outside in the garden area with Robin, Carol and me.

Kris said, "We need to leave."

"We are staying here," I replied.

"I don't think so," said Kris.

This was a glimpse of my strong-willed daughter, and for this I am happy.

This is a day of many visitors. Tifani, Deb Peterson (Kris' high school gymnastics coach), Lana, Ryan, Robin, Carol, Ann, Brad and Josh all stopped by to see her.

Due to such a busy day, she missed sleeping during the day and her daytime tube feeding, ending up with a stomach ache.

This evening, Kris became quite agitated. She kept pulling her clothes out of the closet and packing them in her suitcase. I kept taking them out of the suitcase and putting them back in the closet. She would pull them out again. Finally, she got tired and settled down, but did not sleep well. We assumed it was from all the activity.

AUGUST 7

Every morning, the occupational therapists wake Kris so she can relearn the morning routine of washing, using the bathroom and brushing her teeth. Because Kris can't grasp what needs to be done each morning or in what order it should be done, the therapists start by helping her pick out her clothes. Then they teach her how to use the soap and shampoo, etc.

In other words, the things a healthy person takes for granted are a challenge for Kris. She will go into the bathroom and just stare, because she can't decide which task needs to come first. She gets frustrated, freezes and isn't able to do any of it. Kris used to be so organized, but now even her morning routine is mind-boggling. All these things needed to be relearned, including how to turn on the water faucet and which is hot and which is cold.

Then, out of the blue, we see a flash of the old Kris. When Tif walked into the room today, Kris called her by name.

Today, Kris told us that she couldn't hear. We assume that the illness has caused some hearing loss; another step backwards. All day Kris kept saying she couldn't hear me. She is getting very agitated with not being able to hear us. But one very good thing is she now seems to be able to get herself to the bathroom without us suggesting she needs to use it.

Yes, I sure do like this.

AUGUST 8
SHERRY

I called Kris' room from home this morning because Roger had stayed overnight with her.

His comment: "She was a bearcat."

We all take turns staying overnight with her at the care center, as we are worried about leaving her alone. She is a beautiful young lady who has no street smarts and no knowledge of what is right or wrong.

Finally, today they stopped feeding Kris by the PEG. She had a great day at physical therapy and ran several miles on the treadmill. She also did well at speech therapy.

Roger asked her to match cards and she did it with no problem. He was so proud of her and said, "What a great job!" Kris looked at him and said, "What do you think I am, retarded?" Little did she know how afraid we were that she might never regain her full mental capacity.

Kris also wants the tube out of her stomach, which she calls a "tumor." She keeps saying, "Just cut the cancer out of my stomach and get rid of it."

On a sad note, she is having trouble hearing again.

KRIS

I have a strong memory of the feeding tube. I thought it was a "tumor" in my stomach and wanted it cut out NOW.

AUGUST 9
SHERRY

Kris had a hard night again. This is the fourth night of constant scratching and itching. I'm always wondering what will happen next with this disease.

No tube feeding today, but Kris must eat enough on her own so she doesn't have to go back to those tube feedings. So we have been giving her at least three to four Ensures every day. After a few days of this, she was giving us such dirty looks as if to say, "I hate this but I'll drink it because I don't want that tube in me."

We tell her that if she wants to go outside, she has to drink an Ensure. Since she always wants to be outside, this is another great way to get more calories into her.

She had me bring some of her videos to the care center. Oh, you think she wanted to watch movies? No—we exercised to those videos! Like a three-year-old who has no filter, Kris would point and laugh at me because I could not keep up. Now, you might think I took this with good humor, but the competitive me wanted to tell her to go fly a kite! It was good to see her laughing, though.

Tying her shoes was a large obstacle to overcome. Her dad worked with her many times and was very patient the many times she tried without success.

When the rest of us had had enough and wanted to walk away from the problems, her dad would be patient.

KRIS

I do remember sitting on the edge of the bed with all eyes on me, watching me drink the Ensure. I hated it, but do remember being told it was the "only way I could get the tumor out."

AUGUST 11
SHERRY

Kris was an avid reader before her illness. Now, she's trying so hard to read again by looking at children's books. So today, I gave her my book, *The Life* by Steve Martin. She doesn't seem to want to put it down. Does she understand what she is reading? She must still be struggling, because she asked me to get her a book with larger print.

How strong and determined is our young lady and what obstacles has she yet to conquer? It is so great to see her use her mind again and make decisions for herself.

She went to sit in the lounge, saying, "I'm here because I'm tired of my room." Looking at a magazine, she tore out a page and taped it to her wall. What did it say, you ask? "DON'T WORRY, YOU'VE GOT BILLIONS OF BRAIN CELLS." That became a line we all used for the next couple of years.

AUGUST 12
SHERRY

Roger stayed overnight with Kris so I could sleep. He took vacation this week so he could help stay with her. I was so exhausted from trying to sleep with one eye open to make sure she was okay.

We still could't ever leave Kris alone, as they did not have enough staff to take care of her. In fact, one day Roger tested her to see what she would do if left unattended. Kris left the building and just started walking down the middle of the road, oblivious to the risks. He quickly corralled her and brought her back.

Roger took Kris to see an audiologist at another hospital. They thought the antibiotics may have caused her hearing loss. A new concern—will she ever hear again? I need to just be thankful she is alive.

Roger and Kris jogged for a mile today. Thank goodness that's not my job.

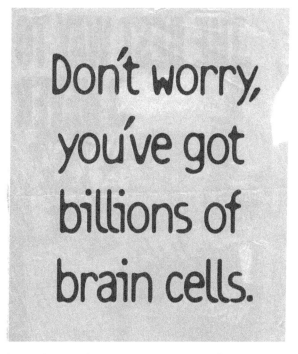

Don't worry, you've got billions of brain cells.

This is the actual page Kris ripped out of the magazine.

AUGUST 13
SHERRY

Kris was angry with me today when I told her she would not be moving home with us yet.

The nurse practitioner and the doctor were in to see Kris and to discuss removing her feeding tube. They suggested giving her a sedative to put her to sleep, but because company was coming later that evening, we decided against it.

What I didn't realize is the feeding tube is like a stopper with the big end inside of her and that it had to be pulled out through a smaller hole. Kris did scream when it came out; I realized that this was the first time she has reacted to pain. At least we don't have to contend with putting more drugs in her body. She had lots of company tonight, including her grandparents.

KRIS

I have some memories of eating lunch at the care center with one of nurses. I remember looking forward to lunchtime; I got to pick out what I wanted to eat. I remember exactly what I ate—every day I got the same thing—a huge slice of pizza (like the gigantic pieces you get at the mall), a large Mountain Dew and a huge brownie.

Nothing had ever tasted so good to me. It was probably just a few times I ate this lunch, but it's a very strong memory.

AUGUST 14
SHERRY

Roger stayed overnight with Kris again. He seems to be able to sleep there and is very patient with Kris.

Today, I checked out Sister Kenny and Courage Center to see which would be best for Kris and which one had an opening. Both have many things to offer, but Sister Kenny is easier to get to with me working.

My brother, Mark, came and brought Kris supper. Lana also visited us with her daughter, Jodi.

Kris is quite angry because she can't hear again. She got a phone call and became very upset because she couldn't hear the person. She said, "I'm just so tired of being sick."

AUGUST 15
SHERRY

Kris is frustrated again this morning. She couldn't get her curling iron cord untangled and got very mad at me when I tried to help her. She expects everything to work the first time she tries it. My Type-A girl doesn't have patience when things don't work for her.

Ever since she was two, she has wanted to do everything herself. We had a discussion about how it hurts me when she gets angry with me. She flashed me her beautiful smile and said she was sorry. Now, remember, when I talk to her I must face her and speak very slowly so she can understand. At times, I have to write it down for her, which frustrates her, as it takes me longer to write it down and then she needs to try to comprehend what I wrote.

To know Kris is to know that patience is not one of her attributes. One of my notes to Kris on her board said, "You are too hard on Kris." She wrote back that she is tired of being here at the center.

Today, I took Kris to see Dr. Penovich; she sees her several times each week, yet she did not recognize her.

AUGUST 16
SHERRY

Roger had overnight duty again. This is the first day since June 11 that I haven't spent some time with Kris. It is a strange feeling. I am still afraid something will happen to Kris when I'm not there.

I still need to learn to trust in God.

AUGUST 17
HOMECOMING
SHERRY

This is the first time since June 11 that Kris is home for a visit and it feels so good. I got tears in my eyes when she walked through the door; I just hadn't known if she would ever come home again.

We went over to Ray and Sharon's house, as Sharon is making Kris' favorite meal of chicken and noodles. It was so good to see her eat several platefuls—she is still well under 100 pounds.

She brought her chalkboard along and requested we answer her questions by writing on the board. Kris actually wrote her first sentence. Prior to that she didn't know the difference between a noun and verb or how to sequence a sentence.

KRIS

I remember being at Sharon's house for chicken and noodles. She had a few tables set up in the living room where we ate. I don't remember who all was there, but I remember being so full that my stomach hurt.

AUGUST 18
SHERRY

Today, Kris went to the hospital for extensive hearing testing, as they were not happy with the earlier tests. They tested her hearing from the inner ear to the brain stem and then tested from the inner ear to the outer ear.

Today's tests determined that Kris doesn't have a hearing

The first visit home during her stay at the care center and before Sister Kenny.

Left - Kris, Mom
Below - Kris, Dad

problem. So what is causing it? Is this only temporary or is this something else she will have to live with?

But let's look at this positively—we were told that many other capabilities would never come back, so maybe with enough work and prayer this, too, can be fixed.

They told us Kris' problem is that her brain hears what we say, but it needs to process the information, think of the answer and then process speaking the answer. This will take lots of patience on everyone's part. Kris is very frustrated and tired from all the testing.

As we were leaving the hospital we walked by the chapel where Roger and I went daily to pray. I asked Kris if she wanted to go to the chapel to pray. She said, "I don't think so, I'm kind of mad at Him right now."

AUGUST 19

Roger stayed overnight again last night. He had Kris call me on the phone and try to talk to me, with no success. We took her out for lunch, as we still cannot get her to eat much at the care center. She is still under 100 pounds and we need her to get healthy. She eats more when we go to a restaurant, which also means we don't have to push her into drinking all that Ensure every day.

Mark, Robin, Ryan and Jake are leaving for vacation so they stopped by to see Kris on their way out of town.

Kris' eyes light up when family and friends stop by to see her.

AUGUST 20

We took Kris to see Dr. Ridley and he talked with Kris about how far she has come. She doesn't remember, but the rest of us can sure see a great deal of improvement, even though there are miles to go.

We called Dr. Penovich's office regarding a prescription change and learned she was out of town until Monday. Now I'm back to being scared, as Dr. Penovich is still my rock in deciding whether we should reduce Kris' prednisone from 40 to 20 milligrams. It is time to be patient again because everyone needs to get away.

AUGUST 21

After consulting with the doctor, we decide that tomorrow we will take Kris out of Lake Ridge Center and head for home. Kris could stay longer at Lake Ridge, as the therapy is very good, but we are all worn out from driving there (an hour's drive each way) and staying every night. I'm already excited about sleeping in my own bed.

On Monday she will start at Sister Kenny.

*Humble yourselves, therefore,
under God's mighty hand,
that he may lift you up in due time.*

Peter 5:6

Chapter 11

Center of the Labyrinth

August 25
Sherry

The next couple of months continued to be difficult, as we still couldn't leave Kris alone. That meant her Grandpa, who is 82, stayed at our home a lot for Kris' safety.

We took her Sister Kenny Rehabilitation Institute, which is widely known for occupational and physical therapy, speech and language pathology and specialty services such as brain injury rehabilitation. They help patients accomplish daily tasks and regain as much independence as possible.

Kris was at Sister Kenny three days a week to learn activities of daily living (ADLs). She needed help with writing, spelling, math and just about everything; Kris wasn't sure if her bra went over or under her shirt.

Will she have to relearn everything or will some of it come back over time? She had to learn how to spell her name. At first she was spelling it Kissss, but she never gave up.

In therapy, they had her doing word-finds and scrambled word sheets. She was working at a second grade level and trying

Kris learning to write again.

diligently to get all of her mental capacity back. When she started using a computer at Sister Kenny, that really seemed to help.

When we first started at Sister Kenny, she needed help finding the therapy room. At the end of her appointment, I would stop by the room and pick her up, as she couldn't find her way down to the entrance of the building. She was not even allowed to walk from one therapy unit to another alone.

Kris started writing poetry as a way to get her feelings on paper and I think that really helped her.

First bike trip after the hospital with mom
and my godmother, Carol Hadac.

OCTOBER

One day, the occupational therapists were teaching Kris basic cooking skills while I watched. They were making mac and cheese, and the noodles in the boiling water were done cooking. They asked what needed to be done next. Kris was starting to pull the noodles out of the boiling water with her bare hands when they stopped her. She still has a lot to learn.

In October, Kris' godmother and I took Kris on a five-mile bike ride to Cannon Falls. On the way back, we couldn't keep up with her and she would not wait. She left us in the dust. We worried until we got back to the car (a mile and a half later) and saw her waiting for us with this big grin on her face. She was so proud of herself for figuring out the way back.

She is starting to look better, but is still deep in the maze.

NOVEMBER 1997

Here we go again! Roger and I were sound asleep upstairs in our bedroom, when we heard Kris hollering for us to come quick. Are the nightmares starting again? Many nights, she wakes up screaming; it is so frightening for her and us. It is always hard to go back to sleep, even though most of the time she has no

memory of what scared her. Roger and I take turns getting up and being with her during these episodes.

It was my turn, so I hollered down the stairs, "I'm coming!" I stood by the door of her bedroom and looked in. I expected her to be afraid, but she was very calm and quiet.

Kris was sitting up and said, "Do you see them?"

I said, "Who do you see?"

She said, "The angels are here. One is over your head by the door and the other one is in this corner. They came to tell me I will be okay. Mom, everything will be okay."

I feel so good and she is smiling. Well, that is good enough for me. Everything will get better; it will just take some time.

DECEMBER 1997-JANUARY 1998

Christmas came with the normal tree expedition.

Kris was improving slowly. She was still seeing Dr. Ridley and Dr. Penovich. Then in January, they started reducing her medications so that she could eventually get off the steroids.

The Christmas after the illness. Left to right, Sherry, Kris & Roger. Kris still wore headbands and hats to hide the loss of her hair.

Kris turned 27 this month and we celebrated with a golf game in the snow on the pond behind our house with family and friends. Her physical ability is back, but we still have a long way to go with her mental capabilities.

I had thought after we got out of the hospital that everything would be back to normal. *This is the new normal: she is alive.*

Many days, Kris is extremely frustrated. So guess who feels her anger? She will be speaking and can't remember a word. So, as a mother, I will tell her the missing word. Sometimes the look I get from her says, "I could just shoot you." I sense her upset that I know the word and she knows the word, but she can't get it out.

For example, she might say, "I want to go for a _____." I try to guess the missing word and suggest "ride." Then she looks at me angrily and tries a word like "water" and I say, "You mean walk." It's worse when I help her in front of others. Here is a very articulate person who now has trouble finding the right words.

MARCH 1998
SHERRY

In March, Kris went downhill skiing in Wyoming. Both Dr. Penovich and Dr. Ridley told her she had to be very careful, as a head injury from a fall could affect her illness. They insisted she wear a helmet, as the incision from the biopsy had not healed yet. We were afraid to let her go, but there is no stopping Kris once she makes up her mind. She acted emotionally and mentally like she was fourteen but she did come home from this trip very proud of herself.

KRIS

I remember skiing and, in particular, that first lift ride to the top. I was so excited I couldn't wait to take off. Everyone was stopping on the way down the hill to check in with each other. I skied all the way down without stopping or looking back and then skied for a time by myself until someone in the group saw me and signaled to the rest that I was fine. This didn't dawn on me as a problem, but I was told later there was considerable concern and I was scolded for not staying with the group.

I don't really remember conversations or interactions during this trip because talking really wasn't my thing at that time; it was still difficult to get the words out. But I definitely remember the physical exhilaration of skiing.

MAY 1998
SHERRY

This month, Kris had a flare-up, indicating her brain function was slowing. The increase in medication seemed to work, as she started moving in the right direction again.

Now she wants to drive—can she even find her way home? She has had a hard time understanding that, due to the seizures, she needs to prove she is fit to drive again. Even talking about the fact frustrates her. Why did we take her license away from her?

And, for that matter, why did she no longer have her car? We sold her car when she was in intensive care as we didn't know if she'd be able to drive again. Plus, we needed the money for medical bills, not car payments. (We did take her to Courage Center where she passed a special driving test.)

JUNE-JULY 1998
SHERRY

That summer—one year after Kris' hospitalization—I really struggled with Kris' whole situation. I kept praying and asking God to be with us. Kris was seeing a psychologist to help her deal with which abilities were and were not coming back to her. I was also seeing a psychologist, as I was having a hard time with what would happen to Kris for the rest of her life. Again, I questioned God and tried to tell Him what we needed. Me of little faith needed to know God was in charge, and to be patient with God's timing and not ours.

I was so happy Kris was alive but sensed her everyday frustrations. It was difficult for her to have patience with herself and her limitations. This was a very intelligent young lady who was now aware enough to realize she wasn't understanding everything that was being said and happening around her.

Plus, the steroids were making Kris break out, gain weight and have terrible mood swings.

Kris started doing several things to stimulate her brain function. Robin and she spent many hours using math flash cards to help her relearn basic arithmetic. Kris also started piano lessons again, something she had done for four years while growing up.

SEPTEMBER 1998
SHERRY

The doctors told us that learning a foreign language is very beneficial to a person with a brain injury. Kris had minored in French in college but couldn't speak or remember any of it. Her high school French teacher, Ms. Ellingson, volunteered to help Kris and started working with her weekly. She would give her worksheets and spend time with her each week speaking the French language.

So many people shared in making Kris whole again.

NOVEMBER 1998
SHERRY

Kris started working at a Target store in Owatonna. This was frustrating for her, as at one time she had worked in the corporate office in downtown Minneapolis. Now it was a challenge for her to work on the floor at a Target store.

One night, she called us in a panic while driving home from Owatonna in a storm. She was crying and not sure what to do. Now, if you know Kris, you know she never called for help before her illness. She was always very confident and could figure out how to handle any problem. But now she had no idea what to do. Roger stayed on the phone with her until the storm had passed.

KRIS

I remember working at the Target store and feeling frustrated and occasionally embarrassed when I recalled that I used to work at the Target corporate office. I don't remember focusing too much on what used to be versus what I had to conquer that day. I think the illness saved me from facing the reality of what normal responsibilities would be for a person my age; I really could only comprehend the next step. Ultimately, I failed at this job because my brain wasn't ready for the multi-tasking required in a 9-to-5 job.

Things were difficult as I became aware that I was different. I wasn't getting the jokes or following the conversations around me. At times, I was vividly aware that people didn't know what to say to me. This was extremely hurtful and made me feel like a complete outsider.

Here I was, a 27-year-old who used to have fun and party with girlfriends and now my days and nights were filled with math flashcards and French lessons.

DECEMBER 1998
SHERRY

At this time, we had several doctor appointments each week. It was a time of trial and error with one medication after another. It was an exhausting time, as we just didn't know how much better she could get. But remember, our Kris posted that magazine page that said, "Don't worry, you've got billions of brain cells."

Kris never settles for where she is at; she always wants more. But, as Dr. Ridley said, "It is her strong will that drives her to improve." Most people would have just given up.

To add to her frustration, Kris was fired from her job. She had never been fired before. I feel her pain, as I'm sure this is very hard on my Type-A girl's self-esteem.

JANUARY–MARCH 1999
SHERRY

Kris' brain function started improving and she was hired at St. Olaf College as a secretary. She worked there for several months and during this time, her brain function continued to improve. I will never forget the day she told me she was quitting that job, as she knew that now she could do her boss's job.

Ah, yes, life is better and it's time to celebrate. Kris is finally getting closer to being her old self, almost two years later.

APRIL 1999
SHERRY

Kris still has down days and life continues to be a struggle, as there are still flare-ups that make it hard for her to concentrate and to work to her full potential. What makes things most difficult is that this disease isn't easy to recognize. Most people look at her and think I'm exaggerating, because she looks fine.

My normally spunky and engaged daughter gets quiet and reserved when her brain is not functioning, so most people don't recognize what is happening. She is very good at covering up when things aren't at one hundred percent, as she doesn't want anyone to know and she generally doesn't want to acknowledge it to herself.

Most of the time life goes quite well, but each year she does have some problems and we worry. I know: "Leave that to God," but aren't we mothers put on this earth to take care of our children?

But those who hope in the LORD
will renew their strength.
They will soar on wings like eagles;
they will run and not grow weary,
they will walk and not be faint.

Isaiah 40:31

Chapter 12

Final Thoughts from Kris

I have a plaque in our house that reads, "Then, when it seems we will never smile again, life comes back." So, I'm okay, after all that. I'm actually much better than okay.

I'm married and have an incredible husband, Ryan, a step-daughter, Dani, and our new Bichon Frise puppy, Louie. My mom is my best friend and I am very close with her and my dad. We spend a lot of time with my parents and my in-laws, playing cards, golfing and visiting. My extended family members are all nearby, so weekends often consist of get-togethers for birthdays, holidays or no special reason at all.

I live with CNS vasculitis daily and take a medicine that suppresses my immune system. This medicine, called Cellcept, is the same medicine a transplant patient takes so their body doesn't reject a new organ. With my vasculitis, my immune system attacks my brain. Nobody knows why, except it's an autoimmune attack.

I still regularly see Dr. Ridley, who has now been taking care of me for over 19 years. We've changed medicines a number of times to determine what works the best with my illness.

Dr. Ridley and me.

Through the years, I've wondered why he casually tells jokes and stories during appointments instead of asking how I'm doing. I've come to realize that he is evaluating me while he is telling jokes. If I "get" the jokes and seem to follow along with the stories, he knows I am doing okay. If I don't, he knows the vasculitis is kicking in.

Through this book-writing process, I thought that talking about what happened would trigger some memories. I'm fascinated by what happened to me during all those lost months but oddly, not one new memory surfaced. It's like a bad dream. I know it happened, but only remember bits and pieces. Strangely though, everyone else can remember what I can't.

The few memories I have from "when I was sick" are distinct and vivid. When it all started, I felt like I was going crazy. I remember having the first seizure while I was running, one night of being locked in the psych ward and the "tumor" in my stomach. I also have a clear recollection of sitting on the side of the bed at the care center while everyone was cheering me on to drink a can of Ensure so we could go outside for a walk.

Several times in the last 19 years, my mom asked if I wanted to read her journal. I would read a little and talk with her, then quickly throw myself back into my "busy" life. I think, because I didn't have a memory of it, it wasn't "real" to me. If I heard too much, it became too real. I was afraid that if I realized how sick I really had been, I would quit moving forward.

I almost died. My heart stopped repeatedly. My entire family came to say goodbye to me, including my grandparents who have since passed. I survived this illness by the grace of God and my family's love and faith.

Recovery is difficult. Books and movies always end when the person lives and then we assume everything is sunshine and roses after that. It's really not. It's not easy to be a 27-year-old re-learning everything, including elementary-level math and reading. There is embarrassment, anger and frustration. There is pride. And there is judgement. When you are emotionally and mentally at a grade school level, your judgement and impulsiveness are far different than that of an adult. You are judged for your behavior as an adult because you look like an adult, but your emotions and behavior are those of an awkward adolescent.

Needless to say, I made it through that. Not without many times giving myself the credit instead of God. Lesson learned again and again…

I think finding a certain balance after illness is really difficult. You can't worry about getting sick again because you'll never live the gift of the present. Likewise, you need to have a certain respect for what happened and some awareness around your limitations.

Unfortunately, I don't seem to know that word "limitations." Consequently, I just about killed myself trying to recover my mental and physical capacities. I went right past "where I was before" and kept going, trying to keep the illness away. I got married, then divorced, then married again. I climbed up the corporate ladder, ran a marathon and competed in fitness competitions for over ten years. Then I had a relapse in November 2015.

Another thing I learned by writing this book is there are different phases in life. Sometimes you need to stop, reassess and go in a different direction, and sometimes it's just time for a new journey.

After the illness: Kris and Grandpa Archie

Grandpa and I had a special relationship. He bandaged my hands, picked me up from day hospital and stayed with me so I wasn't alone.

I met my husband the week before my Grandpa passed in November 2009. I lost a best friend but gained a life-long friend and companion. There are no coincidences.

Focus on your natural strengths; they are, after all, your "spiritual gifts." They say you never work a day in your life if you do what you're passionate about. Isn't it interesting that what you love and are passionate about becomes your gift to the world? Don't get caught up in what you think the world expects or run from something that makes you afraid.

I hope this book helps people in many different ways. I hope your heart is warmed by the power of love, faith and family.

My favorite part of writing has been the excuse to spend time with my mom and dad. For two years now, my mom and I have written together at her house once a week. It probably took two years because we spent as much time visiting over a glass of wine as writing! I believe that was part of the journey.

We weren't intending to write a book about those times. It was more of an effort to help me fill in the gaps for all the time I'd lost and understanding what happened to me while I was sick. I got so much more out of it than that, like the knowledge that we get one chance to build these wonderful memories.

I also hope you love who you are and who God made you to be; there is no other accomplishment or status that can make you as truly happy.

Live in love, laughter and light…

Kris Shuss Kelbrants

Top - Me and my
husband Ryan today.

Left - Ryan and me
with Dani and our
new puppy, Louie.

Ryan's and my wedding in 2012

"When you saw only one set of footprints,

it was then that I carried you."

Footprints by Mary Stevenson

Chapter 13

Final Thoughts from Sherry

So one might think, "Well, she made it through that hard time, so now begins a new life." That is the end of the story in most books and "everyone lives happily ever after."

Over the years, I have watched Kris continue to grow and continue to fight this disease, which seems to grab at her just when it feels like everything is going great.

She has times when she struggles because of this illness. I have seen her still trying to hide the fact that she is not feeling well. She hides it like it is something to be ashamed of. I have seen her go on as if she never had this disease. Until two years ago, when we started the book-writing process, she would never even talk about the illness.

We all have struggles in life and I feel Kris' struggle has made her a stronger person. Kris' faith in God has given her strength when nothing and no one else could. I've seen Kris go from feeling very successful to feeling very insecure during a flare-up. She often doesn't recognize what is happening until she is really struggling.

How has it affected me? It has made my faith stronger, as I know that without God, life lacks meaning and purpose. It has also made me scared, very scared at times. I know I can't control this illness but when I see it sneaking up on her, I want to fight to make sure we never get lost in the maze again. It is still extremely hard for me when I see Kris pushing too much to accomplish something she is determined to do. She is so like me in that she set goals that are difficult to meet. If the normal person accomplishes five things in a day, Kris has to make sure she does ten.

What is the fear level for me? Even though I know I need to trust in the Lord, there are still nights when I worry about losing her. Last year, when she had a major flare-up, it was very difficult for me. We were out of town and when I would talk with her on the phone, I could sense things weren't right, although she didn't want us to worry.

I know I need to trust that God, Kris' husband and Dr. Ridley will keep her safe. Dr. Ridley knows Kris and he knows she will downplay her health concerns. He knows how important daily exercise is and has encouraged her in it. He has told us that if she hadn't been so physically fit, she would not have survived.

He never makes appointments seem like a big deal, but in his own efficient way, he has handled all concerns and situations that have come up in the last 19 years. He listens, absorbs and quietly makes decisions that have allowed Kris to live a full, fruitful life. I dread hearing of the day he will retire.

During one of our meetings with our editor, Kris said she now realizes climbing the corporate ladder and being successful at everything is not the most important thing in life. It is most important to have God, family and be at peace with what she has.

I just looked at both of them and said, "Aha, that's it! That is why I wanted to write this book. I needed Kris to realize that the journey of life is important and not only the arrival."

My goals changed as we went through the maze. When we started, I only wanted to find out what illness Kris had, fix it and get back to our previous lives. Now, my goals are just to have Jesus walk with her and watch for her smiles.

Writing this book has brought us closer and helped us to appreciate the little things in life. I have had the opportunity to share with my daughter memories that were both happy and sad. I think it was important for her to understand her illness and realize what an important part her faith played in her recovery.

Because she is willing to share with others, it is my hope that people who have similar struggles will realize that God doesn't take away the burdens, but He stays with you through them and gives you the courage you need to handle whatever may come your way.

God bless.

Sherry Shuss

About the Authors

Kris Kelbrants lives in Apple Valley, Minnesota with her husband, Ryan. When she isn't writing, she enjoys spending time with her stepdaughter Dani, puppy Louie, family, fitness, golfing, waterskiing, cooking and traveling. Three words that describe Kris are energetic, determined and "a spitfire."

Beating the odds of survival, co-author Kris Kelbrants embarked on writing this book with her mother, Sherry. With few recollection of the most harrowing time of her life, Kris hoped to unlock some missing memories. While no new memories were found, instead, she unearthed something even more valuable—a deepened faith and the opportunity to build an extraordinary bond with her mother.

Sherry Shuss also lives in Apple Valley with her husband of 49 years, Roger. She is enjoying retirement and her first loves are being with family and friends, gardening, golfing and walking.

When the family's world was turned upside down by Kris' sudden illness, a hospital advocate recommended that Sherry keep a daily journal. That journal made it possible to capture the events of Kris' mysterious illness in minute detail.

If you have enjoyed this book or it has touched your life in some way, we invite you to visit MyHealthyAngel.com and follow Kris' blog. She will entertain you with healthy living tips, photos, food, fitness and humor.

Blessings!

CPSIA information can be obtained
at www.ICGtesting.com
Printed in the USA
LVOW05s0758090517

533708LV00048B/1268/P